Keto Diet for Beginners #2019

Simple Keto Recipes to Reset Your Body and Live a Healthy Life (How You Lose 30 Pounds in 21 Days)

Ronda Carlsser

Table of contents

Introduction

This book helps to guide you and understand various aspects about one of the most successful and healthy diets known as the ketogenic diet. In this book, you will learn how to cook nutritious and delicious food at home with minimal effort. Most people follow various diets to reduce weight. The keto diet is one of the best ways to reduce your weight with less effort. The keto diet not only helps to reduce your excess weight but also helps to prevent various afflictions like Alzheimer's disease, epilepsy, Parkinson's disease, and type 2 diabetes.

Home-cooked meals are one of the best ways to consume essential nutrients, which are needed by our body for growth and to perform daily activities. On the other side, fast foods are low in nutritional values and high in calories. In this book, you can see various ketogenic diet benefits and keto-friendly food lists in detail. Adopting the ketogenic diet boosts your energy level naturally and helps you develop healthy eating habits.

Chapter 1: The Basics of the Keto Diet

What is the Keto Diet?

The keto diet is one of the low-carb and high-fat diet plan. It is not just a diet plan but also a healthy habit to consume natural and nutritious foods. It reduces your daily carbohydrate intake and replacing it with fat. Carbohydrates are used as the primary source of energy in your body. When you follow the ketogenic diet, your carb intake is reduced. Due to this, your body uses fat and ketones as a primary source of energy. Ketones are produced when your body burns fat for energy instead of carbs, causing your body to go into a state of ketosis.

Ketosis is the metabolic process in which fats are broken down to produce ketones and energy due to the absence of carbohydrates. The keto diet helps to reduce your weight and provides an endless source of energy to your body. The keto diet is also useful to provide you a better physical and mental health.

How Keto Is Different From Other Diets

- The keto diet is effective for weight loss to compare to any other diet because it burns fat more effectively when your body enters ketosis.
- The keto diet is more restrictive compared to most other diets regarding the intake of carbohydrates.
- Compared to other diets, the keto diet is very effective on various diseases like epilepsy, mental disorder, Parkinson's, high blood pressure, type-2 diabetic, and metabolic syndrome.
- Compared to other diets, the keto diet provides fast and long-term health benefits.
- The keto diet leads to more fat loss and quick improvement in your health compared to other low-carb diets.

How Does the Ketogenic Diet Work?

Glucose is the main primary source of energy in your body. Glucose is produced in your body when carbohydrates are metabolized. This glucose is stored in your body's cells, and excess glucose is converted into glycogens with the help of a chemical process called glycogenesis. These glycogens are reserve source of energy, which is stored in your muscles and liver.

The keto diet is carb-restrictive diet. It reduces the glycogen store and also decreases the insulin level in your body. During this process, fatty acids are released from stored fat in your body, and the liver converts it into ketones. These ketones are used by your body an alternative source of energy. When the ketone level increases, your body pushes into ketosis. When your body is in ketosis, it breaks down fat for energy instead of glucose. The keto diet has numerous health benefits. It not just only helps to reduce your weight but also helps prevent the development of certain diseases.

How to Know When You Are in Ketosis

While on the keto diet, your body undergoes many changes. Below are the various signs and symptoms that show that you are in ketosis:

1. Bad breath: This problem mostly occurs when the ketones level in your body are increased. During the fat-breaking process, acetones are produced and released through the mouth. This result is called keto breath, which commonly occurs for a few days after starting the keto diet. This bad breath is a sign that you are in the state of ketosis.

2. Rapid weight loss: The keto diet is very effective for weight loss. When you start the keto diet, you may notice that your weight decreases rapidly during the first week. Rapid weight loss happens because you start a keto diet and restricts carb intake. This is another sign that you are in the ketosis.

3. Increase urination: You may notice more frequent urination during the first week. This is happening when your body is losing glycogens. When you start a ketogenic diet, the blood glucose level is low in your body. The glycogens contain a great deal

of water, resulting in an increased urge to urinate. Increased urination is another example of toxins releasing from your body.

4. **Increased thirst and dry mouth:** During the keto diet, while your body is in ketosis, there is a need for an excess number of glycogens. During this process, urination occurs more frequently, created increase your thirst. Another reason for thirst and dry mouth is that the decrease in insulin level in your body allows your kidneys to release water and sodium. This is another sign that you are in the ketosis.

5. **High energy level:** When you are in ketosis, your energy level increases as does your concentration. You can feel energized throughout the day — both physically and mentally.

The Health Benefits of the Keto Diet

The ketogenic diet has various health benefits, including the following:

1. **Weight loss:** The keto diet is highly effective on weight loss, making it one of its major benefits. When you are on the keto diet, your carb intake is reduced, your body goes into ketosis and breaks down fat for energy instead of glucose. Research proves that the keto diet is very effective on weight loss to compare to any other diet.

2. **Improves your brain functions:** Ketones are one of the most powerful sources of energy used by your brain. Ketones provide about 70 percent of the energy your brain needs. It helps improve your brain health and also improves memory functions, focus, and attention. Ketones also work as a neuroprotective antioxidant. It helps to prevent your brain cells from harmful reactive oxygen species.

3. **Controls blood sugar level:** Starchy and sugary foods are responsible for increasing your blood sugar level. While on the keto diet, your carbohydrate intake is very low. Due to this, blood sugar levels are lower than normal. Reducing carbohydrate intake in your diet will help you to stabilize your blood sugar level.

4. **Increases energy level:** When fat molecules are broken down for energy, it produces three times more energy compared to carbohydrates. This is one of the

reasons the keto diet gives you both instant and long-lasting energy. It keeps you fully energized for the entire day.

5. Reduces the risk of various diseases: The keto diet is very effective for patients with epilepsy, which is one of the brain disorders related to the central nervous system. Being on this diet can also protect it from metabolic syndromes, high blood pressure, type-2 diabetes, obesity, Parkinson's, and reduce the risk of heart-related diseases. Research also shows that a keto diet is effective on certain cancers.

6. Increase your lifespan: Researchers says that the keto diet helps you to live longer. A recent study conducted that a low-carb diet can help to increase your lifespan. While on the keto diet, you consume healthy food, which is full of nutrients and antioxidants. The keto diet protects us from various health-related problems which are associated with a poor diet. It also helps to reduce the risk of heart disease, obesity, and diabetes.

7. Improves cholesterol levels: Almost everyone knows about high-density lipoprotein (HDL) and low-density lipoprotein (LDL) cholesterol. HDL is popularly known as good cholesterol while LDL is known as bad cholesterol. The keto diet is a low-carb, high-fat diet. A high-fat diet helps to improve the good cholesterol (HDL) level in the body and helps to lower the risk of a heart attack. Carbohydrates are the main cause of the increase in bad cholesterol (LDL) level. The keto diet requires those following it to consume fewer carbohydrates, helping to decrease the bad cholesterol level in the body.

7 Helpful Tips for the Keto Journey

1. Reduce your daily carb consumption: Always keep in mind that the keto diet is a low-carb diet. Eating low-carb food will help you in achieving ketosis. Your body stores excess glucose in your liver and muscle tissue. When your carb intake is low, your body breaks fat for energy. This allows for the release of fatty acids, which the liver converts into ketones.

2. Increase healthy fat intake: People following the keto diet consume plenty of fat, which helps you to boost your ketone levels and help your body reach ketosis. You can consume good fat like avocado oil, coconut oil, and olive oil to achieve this.

3. Regular exercise: During the keto diet, regular exercise helps to increase the ketone level in your body. Your body goes into ketosis and turns fats into energy. This helps to reduce your weight and balance your blood sugar level. It helps you to stay energized throughout the day.

4. Stay hydrated: Drinking plenty of water helps you to stay hydrated and detoxify your body. During the keto diet, your body needs more water, which plays an important role in your body's processes like digestion. You can drink tea, coffee, and smoothies in the morning time, and then drink plenty of water during the remainder of the day.

5. Consume adequate protein intake: The keto diet is very effective for weight loss. During the weight-loss process, the body typically loses both fat and muscle. When you are on a low-carb diet, you have to consume a sufficient amount of protein to help to preserve your muscle mass. Consuming less than the proper amount of protein leads to muscle mass loss while too much protein will affect ketone production.

6. Add coconut oil into your diet: Coconut oil contains a fat called medium chain triglycerides (MCTs). Compared to other fats, MCTs are absorbed quickly and go directly into the liver. The liver can convert it into ketones immediately. MCT provides a quick source of energy to your body because it is metabolized easily and immediately into ketone bodies. It also helps to reduce digestive side effects like stomach cramping.

7. Get enough sleep: While you are on the ketogenic diet, your body needs enough sleep. Getting inadequate sleep will increase your cravings for carbs and also affect the weight-loss process. You should sleep in a dark room in a cool environment. The room temperature is around 65 degrees Fahrenheit, and you should get between seven and eight hours of sleep every night. Good quality sleep will allow you to be energized completely the next day.

Chapter 2: Foods to Eat

Listed below are some of the recommended foods that you can enjoy on the ketogenic diet:

- **Meat:** You can eat all types of meat that are low in carbohydrates. Try to use unprocessed meat because these meats are keto-friendly and low in carbohydrates. Organic and grass-fed meats are healthy choices for those on a keto diet. Use an adequate amount of protein because excess protein converts to glucose.
    - o **All meats:** Ground beef, ground pork, steak, goat, turkey, pork loin, pork chops, lamb, roasts, stew meats, and so on.

- **Fish and seafood:** Fish are one of the best sources of high-quality protein. It is also providing vitamin D and essential fatty acids omega-3. Fatty fish and wild-caught fish and seafood are the best choices for the keto diet. You can usually make healthy fish or seafood dishes in 30 minutes or less.
    - o **Fish:** Catfish, tuna, salmon, cod, flounder, and mackerel.
    - o **Seafood:** Crab, lobster, oysters, squid, scallop, clams, and mussels.

- **Eggs:** Eggs are one of the healthiest foods you can consume while on the keto diet. It is low in carbs and provides an adequate amount of protein for your body.
    - o **Eggs:** Organic and pasteurized eggs are the healthiest choices when following the keto diet.

- **Fruits and vegetables:** Fruits and vegetables are great sources of vitamins and essential nutrients. Leafy, green vegetables are a terrific choice for the keto diet. Most vegetables are low in carbohydrates and add flavor and color to your keto meals. Avoid starchy vegetables. Also, keep in mind that most of the fruits are high in carbs.
    - o **Vegetables:** Spinach, bell peppers, asparagus, broccoli, zucchini, kale, cucumber, chives, avocado, cauliflower, green beans, lettuce, garlic, Brussels sprouts, celery, tomatoes, onion, cabbage, eggplant, and artichokes.
    - o **Fruits:** Avocadoes, coconut, olives, raspberries, blackberries, tomatoes, strawberries, and lemons.
- **Fats and oils:** The keto diet is dependent mostly on healthy fats. Eating the right fats is very important while you are on the keto diet. Healthy fat contains omega-3 and omega-6 fatty acids. Essential fatty acids are an important part of the diet

because your body cannot produce them. While on the keto diet, about 70 to 80 percent of energy comes from fat.

- o Fats and oil: Coconut oil, palm kernel oil, butter, beef fat, olive oil, lard, macadamia nut oil, and avocado oil.

- Dairy products: Keto is more restrictive when it comes to dairy because most of the dairy product contains carbs. Keto mostly recommends full-fat dairy items. Always use hard cheese because it contains lower carbs than soft cheese.
  - o Dairy: Butter, hard cheese, whipping cream, cream cheese, and Greek yogurt.

- Condiments and beverages: Beverages keep you hydrated while condiments can make your food items taste better.
  - o Condiments: Mayonnaise, hot sauce, lemon juice, vinegar, and soy sauce.
  - o Beverages: Plain water, carbonated water, tea, coffee, kombucha, bone broth, smoothie, coconut water, and nondairy milk.

Chapter 3: Foods to Avoid

- Sugary foods: Completely avoid sweeteners from the keto diet because it raises your blood sugar and also causes insulin spikes, which can kick you out from the process of ketosis. Avoid sugary foods like cake, ice cream, fruit juice, soda, candy, chocolate bars, soft drinks, sports drinks, and energy drinks. Also avoid salad dressings, ketchup, and prepackaged food because they contain hidden sugars. Avoid maple syrup and honey because they contain sugars.

- Grains: Cutting out grains from your daily diet is the most important step to reaching ketosis. Grains like wheat, oats, rye, corn, barley, sprouted grains, and buckwheat. Also, avoid products that are made from grains like bread, pasta, crackers, cookies, pizza, and so on.

- Starchy foods: Starchy foods contains carbohydrates that you should avoid these foods during the keto diet. This includes food like potatoes, rice, bread, and pasta.

- Fruits and juices: Most fruits are high in sugar and carbohydrates, such as banana, pineapples, grapes, mangoes, and tangerines. Fruit juices are to be completely avoided while on the keto diet because they contain natural sugar and added sugar.

- Processed foods: Processed foods contain added preservatives, carrageenan, sulfite, hidden sugars, and carbs, so try to avoid them completely from your diet. Avoid processed meat, processed vegetables, and prepackaged foods.

- Refined oil and fats: Avoid unhealthy trans fats from your diet. Polyunsaturated fats are known as a bad fat while on the keto diet as well. Avoid hydrogenated oils, which are found in processed food products like margarine, crackers, and other foods. Processed oils like sunflower oil, soybean oils, canola oils, and safflower oil.

- Artificial sweeteners: Artificial sweeteners often cause food cravings, so eliminate them from your diet. These sweeteners include those with aspartame, sucralose, and saccharine.

Chapter 4: FAQs

How can I know that I am in ketosis?

There are some signs like breath that smells like nail polish remover, an increase in thirst and dry mouth, increase urination and rapid weight loss, all of which can be an indication that your body is in the state of ketosis.

How should I track my ketone level?

There are two methods to track ketones> One process is using urine test strips called keto strips. This is an inexpensive method to track ketone levels. Another method is a blood test, which is one of the most accurate methods to track your ketone levels. This method is expensive, however, and you need a keto meter and keto trips to track your blood ketone level.

How does ketosis work in my body?

When we consume low-carb foods, our body uses fat as a primary energy source. Ketosis is the state in which your liver creates molecules known as ketones. These ketones are used by our body for energy. In this state, your body breaks down fats for energy.

Is a keto diet being safe for people with diabetes?

The keto diet helps to control blood sugar levels. The keto diet is a low-carb diet that doesn't raise your blood sugar level, making it safe for diabetics to follow.

Can I eat fruit on the keto diet?

Most fruits are high in carbs, so you have to consume fruits that are low in carbs like you can eat avocados, coconut, olives, blackberries, raspberries, lemons, and tomatoes.

How long it takes to get me into ketosis?

When you start the keto diet, it normally takes up to seven days to enter in the state of ketosis. This time period is depending upon your eating habits, your body type, and your daily activity levels. Exercising on an empty stomach is one of the most effective, fastest ways to enter ketosis.

Chapter 5: Meal Plan

Week One Meal Plan

Day 1

- Breakfast-Cauliflower Bacon Cheese Casserole
- Lunch-Beef Bowl
- Dinner-Flavors Chicken Tenders

Day 2

- Breakfast-Delicious Broccoli Frittata
- Lunch-Tomato Lemon Fish Fillet
- Dinner-Cabbage Coconut Soup

Day 3

- Breakfast-Easy Overnight Oats
- Lunch-Beef Stew
- Dinner-Mustard Chicken Tenders

Day 4

- Breakfast-Egg Breakfast Muffins
- Lunch-Turmeric Coconut Shrimp
- Dinner-Delicious Ground Beef

Day 5

- Breakfast-Healthy Zucchini Muffins
- Lunch-Garlic Avocado Soup
- Dinner-Chipotle Beef Brisket

Day 6

- Breakfast-Cinnamon Flax Waffles

- Lunch-Chicken Chili
- Dinner-Rosemary Lemon Salmon

Day 7

- Breakfast-Healthy Spinach Muffins
- Lunch-Beef Barbacoa
- Dinner-Spicy Chicken Curry

Week Two Meal Plan

Day 1

- Breakfast-Perfect Broccoli Hash Browns
- Lunch-Spinach Cauliflower Green Soup
- Dinner-Spicy Lamb Chops

Day 2

- Breakfast-Healthy Spinach Muffins
- Lunch-Healthy Turmeric Broccoli Soup
- Dinner-Chicken Cheese Casserole

Day 3

- Breakfast-Cinnamon Flax Waffles
- Lunch-Roasted Mushrooms
- Dinner-Tomato Lemon Fish Fillet

Day 4

- Breakfast-Healthy Zucchini Muffins
- Lunch-Shrimp and Grits
- Dinner-Tasty Pork Tenderloin

Day 5

- Breakfast-Egg Breakfast Muffins
- Lunch-Parmesan Salmon
- Dinner-Lemon Pork Cutlet

Day 6

- Breakfast-Easy Overnight Oats
- Lunch-Chili Lemon Salmon
- Dinner-Moist Shredded Pork

Day 7

- Breakfast-Delicious Broccoli Frittata
- Lunch-Chicken With Mushrooms
- Dinner-Spicy Beef

Week Three Meal Plan

Day 1

- Breakfast-Egg Breakfast Muffins
- Lunch-Beef Bowl
- Dinner-Herb Chicken

Day 2

- Breakfast-Easy Overnight Oats
- Lunch-Tomato Lemon Fish Fillet
- Dinner-Garlic Avocado Soup

Day 3

- Breakfast-Delicious Broccoli Frittata
- Lunch-Spicy Lamb Chops
- Dinner-Chicken Cumin Wings

Day 4

- Breakfast-Cauliflower Bacon Cheese Casserole
- Lunch-Ginger Lime Salmon
- Dinner-Garlic Zucchini Chicken Casserole

Day 5

- Breakfast-Healthy Zucchini Muffins
- Lunch-Chicken Chili
- Dinner-Parmesan Salmon

Day 6

- Breakfast-Cinnamon Flax Waffles
- Lunch-Spinach Cauliflower Green Soup
- Dinner-Lamb Roast

Day 7

- Breakfast-Healthy Spinach Muffins
- Lunch-Shrimp Scampi
- Dinner-Tomato Lemon Fish Fillet

Chapter 6: Breakfast

Cauliflower Bacon Cheese Casserole

Preparation Time: 10 minutes

Cooking Time: 45 minutes

Serve: 6

Ingredients:

- 10 eggs
- 4 cups cauliflower rice
- 10 ounces bacon, cooked and crumbled
- ½ cup heavy cream
- 1 teaspoon paprika
- 8 ounces cheddar cheese, shredded
- ¼ teaspoon ground black pepper
- ½ teaspoon salt

Directions:

1. Preheat the oven to 350F/180C.
2. Spray 2-quart casserole dish with cooking spray and set aside.
3. Spread cauliflower rice evenly into the casserole dish.
4. Spread half shredded cheese on top of cauliflower rice.
5. In a bowl, whisk together eggs, heavy cream, paprika, black pepper, and salt.
6. Pour egg mixture over cauliflower and cheese layer.
7. Sprinkle remaining cheese and bacon on top.
8. Bake in preheated oven for 45 minutes or until eggs are set.
9. Serve and enjoy.

Nutritional Value (Amount per Serving):

- Calories 565

- Fat 43.4 g
- Carbohydrates 5.8 g
- Sugar 2.4 g
- Protein 37.7 g
- Cholesterol 378 mg

Delicious Broccoli Frittata

Preparation Time: 10 minutes

Cooking Time: 20 minutes

Serve: 8

Ingredients:

- 12 eggs
- 2 cups broccoli florets
- 1 garlic clove, minced
- 1 small onion, diced
- 2 tablespoons butter
- 1 cup cheddar cheese, shredded
- ½ cup heavy cream
- ⅛ teaspoon ground black pepper
- ¼ teaspoon salt

Directions:

1. Preheat the oven to 350F/180C.
2. In a bowl, whisk together eggs, heavy cream, black pepper, and salt until well combined.
3. Stir in shredded cheddar cheese and set aside.
4. Melt butter in a large pan over medium heat.
5. Add garlic, onion, and broccoli to the pan and cook for 3 to 4 minutes or until tender.
6. Pour egg mixture into the pan and cook for a minute.
7. Place pan in preheated oven and cook for 13 to 15 minutes.
8. Slice and serve.

Nutritional Value (Amount per Serving):

- Calories 215

- Fat 17 g
- Carbohydrates 3.4 g
- Sugar 1.4 g
- Protein 12.8 g
- Cholesterol 278 mg

Easy Overnight Oats

Preparation Time: 5 minutes

Cooking Time: 5 minutes

Serve: 2

Ingredients:

- 1½ teaspoons chia seeds
- 1½ tablespoons almond butter
- ⅓ cup unsweetened almond milk
- 5 tablespoons hemp seeds

Directions:

1. Add all ingredients in a glass jar and stir well.
2. Place in refrigerator overnight.
3. Stir well and serve.

Nutritional Value (Amount per Serving):

- Calories 194
- Fat 16.5 g
- Carbohydrates 4.2 g
- Sugar 0.5 g
- Protein 9.4 g
- Cholesterol 0 mg

Egg Breakfast Muffins

Preparation Time: 10 minutes

Cooking Time: 25 minutes

Serve: 6

Ingredients:

- 5 eggs
- 2 tablespoons green onion, chopped
- 3 ounces bacon, cooked and chopped
- 1 teaspoon paprika
- 2 tablespoons Parmesan cheese, shredded
- ½ teaspoon ground black pepper
- ¼ teaspoon sea salt

Directions:

1. Spray a muffin tray with cooking spray and set aside.
2. In a bowl, whisk eggs with paprika, black pepper, and salt.
3. Add green onion, cheese, and bacon to the egg mixture and stir well.
4. Pour egg mixture into the prepared muffin tray and bake at 350F/176 C for 20 to 25 minutes.
5. Serve and enjoy.

Nutritional Value (Amount per Serving):

- Calories 135
- Fat 9.9 g
- Carbohydrates 1 g
- Sugar 0.4 g
- Protein 10.3 g
- Cholesterol 153 mg

Healthy Zucchini Muffins

Preparation Time: 10 minutes

Cooking Time: 30 minutes

Serve: 8

Ingredients:

- 1 zucchini, grated
- ½ cup walnuts, chopped
- ½ teaspoon baking soda
- ½ cup coconut flour
- 1 cup almond flour
- 1½ teaspoons ground cinnamon
- ¾ cup unsweetened applesauce
- ¼ cup coconut oil, melted
- 15 drops liquid stevia
- ⅛ teaspoon salt

Directions:

1. Preheat the oven to 325F/162C.
2. Spray a muffin tray with cooking spray and set aside.
3. Add grated zucchini, coconut oil, and stevia to the bowl and mix well.
4. In another bowl, mix coconut flour, baking soda, almond flour, walnuts, cinnamon, and salt.
5. Add zucchini mixture into the coconut flour mixture and mix well.
6. Add applesauce and stir until well combined.
7. Pour batter into the prepared muffin tray and bake in preheated oven for 25 to 30 minutes.
8. Serve and enjoy.

Nutritional Value (Amount per Serving):

- Calories 229
- Fat 18.9 g
- Carbohydrates 12.5 g
- Sugar 3.4 g
- Protein 5.2 g
- Cholesterol 0 mg

Cinnamon Flax Waffles

Preparation Time: 10 minutes

Cooking Time: 10 minutes

Serve: 8

Ingredients:

- 2 cups ground golden flaxseed
- 1 tablespoon gluten-free baking powder
- 10 teaspoons ground chia seed
- 15 tablespoons warm water
- 2 teaspoons ground cinnamon
- ⅓ cup coconut oil, melted
- ½ cup water
- 1 teaspoon sea salt

Directions:

1. Heat waffle iron on medium heat.
2. In a small bowl, mix ground chia seed and warm water.
3. In a large bowl, mix ground flaxseed, sea salt, and baking powder. Set aside.
4. Add melted coconut oil, chia seed mixture, and water into the blender and blend for 30 seconds.
5. Transfer coconut oil mixture into the flaxseed mixture and mix well.
6. Add cinnamon and stir well.
7. Scoop waffle mixture into the hot waffle iron and cook on each side for 3 to 5 minutes or until lightly golden brown.
8. Serve and enjoy.

Nutritional Value (Amount per Serving):

- Calories 240
- Fat 20.6 g

- Carbohydrates 12.9 g
- Sugar 0 g
- Protein 7 g
- Cholesterol 0 mg

Healthy Spinach Muffins

Preparation Time: 10 minutes

Cooking Time: 20 minutes

Serve: 6

Ingredients:

- 6 eggs
- 2 green onions, sliced
- ⅓ cup cheddar cheese, shredded
- ⅓ cup tomatoes, chopped
- ½ cup fresh spinach, chopped
- ¼ cup almond milk

Directions:

1. Preheat the oven to 350F/180C.
2. Spray a muffin tray with cooking spray and set aside.
3. In a mixing bowl, whisk eggs with milk, black pepper, and salt.
4. Stir in green onions, cheese, tomatoes, and spinach.
5. Pour mixture in a prepared muffin tray and bake in preheated oven for 20 minutes.
6. Serve and enjoy.

Nutritional Value (Amount per Serving):

- Calories 115
- Fat 8.9 g
- Carbohydrates 1.8 g
- Sugar 1.1 g
- Protein 7.6 g
- Cholesterol 170 mg

Perfect Broccoli Hash Browns

Preparation Time: 10 minutes

Cooking Time: 20 minutes

Serve: 12

Ingredients:

- 1 egg
- ¼ teaspoon garlic powder
- ¼ teaspoon onion powder
- 4 ounces cheddar cheese, shredded
- 3 cups broccoli rice
- 3 cups cauliflower rice
- Ground black pepper
- Salt

Directions:

1. Preheat the oven to 400F/200C.
2. Add broccoli rice and cauliflower rice in microwave-safe bowl and microwave for 6 minutes.
3. Pour vegetable rice onto a kitchen towel and squeeze out all excess liquid.
4. Return vegetable rice in a bowl. Add egg, garlic powder, onion powder, cheese, black pepper, and salt and mix well to combine.
5. Make 12 evenly shaped patties from vegetable rice mixture and place on a baking tray.
6. Bake in preheated oven for 10 minutes.
7. Turn to another side and cook for 10 minutes more or until golden brown.
8. Serve and enjoy.

Nutritional Value (Amount per Serving):

- Calories 115

- Fat 7.2 g
- Carbohydrates 6.2 g
- Sugar 2.2 g
- Protein 7.9 g
- Cholesterol 47 mg

Chapter 7: Appetizers & Snacks

Perfect Guacamole

Preparation Time: 10 minutes

Cooking Time: 5 minutes

Serve: 8

Ingredients:

- 1 tablespoon fresh lime juice
- 2 avocados, halved and pitted
- 2 tablespoons fresh cilantro, chopped
- 4 tablespoons jalapeno pepper, chopped
- ¼ small onion, chopped
- ½ teaspoon sea salt

Directions:

1. Add cilantro, onion, black pepper, and salt in a food processor and process into a smooth paste.
2. Scoop out the avocado flesh into a bowl and mash with a fork.
3. Add cilantro paste and lime juice and stir to combine.
4. Serve and enjoy.

Nutritional Value (Amount per Serving):

- Calories 104
- Fat 9.8 g
- Carbohydrates 4.7 g
- Sugar 0.4 g
- Protein 1 g
- Cholesterol 0 mg

Delicious Cheese Pepperoni Chips

Preparation Time: 10 minutes

Cooking Time: 10 minutes

Serve: 2

Ingredients:

- 1 ounce pepperoni
- ½ teaspoon Italian seasoning
- 4 tablespoons mozzarella cheese, shredded
- 2 tablespoons Parmesan cheese, grated

Directions:

1. Preheat the oven to 400F/200C.
2. Line baking tray with parchment paper.
3. Place pepperoni on a prepared baking tray.
4. Sprinkle with Parmesan cheese, Italian seasoning, and mozzarella cheese.
5. Bake in preheated oven for 10 minutes.
6. Serve and enjoy.

Nutritional Value (Amount per Serving):

- Calories 271
- Fat 18.8 g
- Carbohydrates 2.1 g
- Sugar 0.1 g
- Protein 22.2 g
- Cholesterol 53 mg

Spicy Cheese Dips

Preparation Time: 10 minutes

Cooking Time: 5 minutes

Serve: 14

Ingredients:

- 4 ounces cream cheese
- ¼ teaspoon garlic powder
- ¼ teaspoon onion powder
- ½ teaspoon lemon juice
- ½ teaspoon Worcestershire sauce
- ½ tablespoon vinegar
- 1 tablespoon fresh parsley, chopped
- 1½ tablespoons sambal oelck
- 2½ tablespoons pimentos
- 2 cups cheddar cheese, shredded
- 2 cups pepper jack cheese, shredded

Directions:

1. Add all ingredients into the mixing bowl and mix until well combined.
2. Serve and enjoy.

Nutritional Value (Amount per Serving):

- Calories 101
- Fat 8.2 g
- Carbohydrates 2.2 g
- Sugar 1.2 g
- Protein 4.9 g
- Cholesterol 26 mg

Tasty Sausage Balls

Preparation Time: 10 minutes

Cooking Time: 20 minutes

Serve: 10

Ingredients:

- 1 egg
- 1 garlic clove, chopped
- ½ onion, chopped
- 1 cup spinach, chopped
- ½ cup Parmesan cheese, grated
- ½ cup mozzarella cheese, shredded
- 1 pound sausage
- 1 teaspoon salt

Directions:

1. Preheat the oven to 400F/200C.
2. Line baking tray with parchment paper and set aside.
3. Add all ingredients in mixing bowl and mix until well combined.
4. Make balls from mixture and place on a baking tray.
5. Bake in preheated oven for 15 to 20 minutes or until cooked through.
6. Serve and enjoy.

Nutritional Value (Amount per Serving):

- Calories 197
- Fat 15.4 g
- Carbohydrates 0.8 g
- Sugar 0.3 g
- Protein 12.3 g
- Cholesterol 61 mg

Crunchy Chive Crackers

Preparation Time: 10 minutes

Cooking Time: 10 minutes

Serve: 4

Ingredients:

- 1 egg
- 2 tablespoons butter
- 2 tablespoons chives
- 4 tablespoons coconut flour
- ¼ cup almond flour
- 2 tablespoons sour cream
- 1¾ cup mozzarella cheese, shredded
- ⅛ teaspoon salt

Directions:

1. Preheat the oven to 400F/200C.
2. Line baking tray with parchment paper and set aside.
3. Melt cheese in a pan over medium heat.
4. Remove pan from heat. Add sour cream and stir to combine.
5. In a bowl, add almond flour, chives, egg, coconut flour, and cheese mixture and mix until well combined.
6. Wrap prepared dough using plastic wrap and place in the refrigerator for 15 minutes.
7. Roll dough between two parchment paper pieces.
8. Using sharp knife cut rolled dough into cracker shapes and place onto a prepared baking tray. Brush with melted butter.
9. Sprinkle with salt and bake in preheated oven for 8 to 10 minutes.
10. Serve and enjoy.

Nutritional Value (Amount per Serving):

- Calories 215
- Fat 15.8 g
- Carbohydrates 10.4 g
- Sugar 1.4 g
- Protein 8.7 g
- Cholesterol 65 mg

Flavorful Spinach Dip

Preparation Time: 10 minutes

Cooking Time: 10 minutes

Serve: 10

Ingredients:

- 10 ounces frozen spinach, chopped
- ½ cup jicama, peeled and diced
- ½ teaspoon erythritol
- 1 teaspoon dried dill weed
- 2 teaspoons dried parsley
- 1 teaspoon onion flakes, minced
- 1 teaspoon onion powder
- 1 teaspoon garlic powder
- 15 ounces sour cream
- ¼ teaspoon ground black pepper
- ½ teaspoon salt

Directions:

1. In a bowl, mix sour cream, erythritol, dill, parsley, onion flakes, onion powder, garlic powder, black pepper, and salt.
2. Drain excess water from spinach.
3. Add jicama and spinach to the cream mixture and mix until well combined.
4. Place in refrigerator for 1 hour.
5. Serve and enjoy.

Nutritional Value (Amount per Serving):

- Calories 103
- Fat 9 g
- Carbohydrates 4.2 g

- Sugar 0.5 g
- Protein 2.3 g
- Cholesterol 19 mg

Shrimp Artichoke Dip

Preparation Time: 10 minutes

Cooking Time: 40 minutes

Serve: 20

Ingredients:

- 12 ounces artichoke hearts, frozen and defrosted
- 1½ teaspoons Old Bay seasoning
- 8 ounces salad shrimp, peeled
- 1 tablespoon Worcestershire sauce
- ½ cup green onion, diced
- ½ cup sour cream
- 8 ounces cream cheese

Directions:

1. Add cream cheese, seasoning, Worcestershire sauce, green onion, and sour cream into the food processor and process until smooth.
2. Add artichoke into the food processor and process twice.
3. Transfer mixture into the bowl.
4. Add shrimp and stir well.
5. Add shrimp mixture into the slow cooker and cook on low for 40 minutes.
6. Stir well and serve.

Nutritional Value (Amount per Serving):

- Calories 72
- Fat 5.3 g
- Carbohydrates 2.7 g
- Sugar 0.4 g
- Protein 4.1 g
- Cholesterol 37 mg

Lemon Cauliflower Hummus

Preparation Time: 10 minutes

Cooking Time: 15 minutes

Serve: 6

Ingredients:

- 3 cups cauliflower florets
- 1½ tablespoons tahini paste
- 2 tablespoons avocado oil
- 2 tablespoons water
- 3 tablespoons olive oil
- 2 garlic cloves, crushed
- 3 tablespoons fresh lemon juice
- ½ teaspoon salt

Directions:

1. In a microwave-safe dish, mix cauliflower florets, garlic cloves, avocado oil, water, and salt, and microwave for 15 minutes or until softened.
2. Transfer cauliflower mixture into the blender and blend.
3. Add remaining ingredients and blend until smooth.
4. Serve and enjoy.

Nutritional Value (Amount per Serving):

- Calories 104
- Fat 9.7 g
- Carbohydrates 4.2 g
- Sugar 1.4 g
- Protein 1.8 g
- Cholesterol 0 mg

Easy Peanut Butter Dip

Preparation Time: 5 minutes

Cooking Time: 5 minutes

Serve: 6

Ingredients:

- ½ cup peanut butter
- ⅓ cup unsweetened cashew milk
- 1 teaspoon vanilla extract
- 35 stevia drops

Directions:

1. Add all ingredients in a bowl and mix until well combined.
2. Serve and enjoy.

Nutritional Value (Amount per Serving):

- Calories 130
- Fat 10.9 g
- Carbohydrates 4.4 g
- Sugar 2.1 g
- Protein 5.4 g
- Cholesterol 0 mg

Zucchini Dip

Preparation Time: 5 minutes

Cooking Time: 5 minutes

Serve: 6

Ingredients:

- 1 zucchini, diced
- ½ cup olive oil
- 2 garlic cloves
- ½ cup sunflower seeds
- 2 tablespoons salt

Directions:

1. Add all ingredients into the blender and blend until smooth.
2. Serve and enjoy.

Nutritional Value (Amount per Serving):

- Calories 173
- Fat 18.8 g
- Carbohydrates 2.2 g
- Sugar 0.7 g
- Protein 1.3 g
- Cholesterol 0 mg

Chapter 8: Beef, Pork & Lamb

Beef Bowl

Preparation Time: 10 minutes

Cooking Time: 15 minutes

Serve: 4

Ingredients:

- 1 pound ground beef
- 15 drops liquid stevia
- 4 garlic cloves, minced
- 2 tablespoons soy sauce
- ¼ tablespoon ginger, grated
- ¼ cup sesame oil
- ¼ cup green onion, chopped

Directions:

1. Heat oil in a large pan over medium heat.
2. Add onion to the pan and sauté until softened.
3. Add meat to the pan and cook for 8 minutes.
4. Add soy sauce, stevia, garlic, and ginger to the pan and simmer for 2 to 3 minutes.
5. Garnish with green onion and serve.

Nutritional Value (Amount per Serving):

- Calories 343
- Fat 20.8 g
- Carbohydrates 2.3 g
- Sugar 0.3 g
- Protein 35.2 g
- Cholesterol 101 mg

Beef Stew

Preparation Time: 15 minutes

Cooking Time: 1 hour, 45 minutes

Serve: 10

Ingredients:

- 3 pounds beef stew meat
- 1 tablespoon fresh parsley, chopped
- ¼ teaspoon thyme
- ¼ teaspoon dried basil
- 1 teaspoon onion powder
- 1 teaspoon garlic powder
- 5 cups water
- 2 cups vegetable juice
- 4 cups beef stock
- 14-ounce can diced tomatoes
- 1 cauliflower head, cut into florets
- 2 celery stalks, chopped
- 8 ounces mushrooms, sliced
- 2 garlic cloves, minced
- ½ onion, chopped
- ¼ cup olive oil
- 1½ tablespoons sea salt

Directions:

1. Heat oil in a large stockpot over high heat.
2. Add garlic and onion to the pot and sauté until softened.
3. Add meat and cook for 10 minutes.
4. Add remaining ingredients and stir well and cook over high heat for 30 minutes.
5. Turn heat to low and simmer for 1 hour or until meat and vegetables are tender.

6. Serve and enjoy.

Nutritional Value (Amount per Serving):

- Calories 337
- Fat 13.9 g
- Carbohydrates 7.7 g
- Sugar 4.4 g
- Protein 44.5 g
- Cholesterol 122 mg

Delicious Ground Beef

Preparation Time: 10 minutes

Cooking Time: 30 minutes

Serve: 8

Ingredients:

- 2 pounds ground beef
- 1 cup water
- 2 tablespoons tomato paste
- ⅓ cup tomatoes, chopped
- ¼ teaspoon cinnamon
- 1 bay leaf
- ¼ cup white wine
- 1 tablespoon butter
- 1 tablespoon olive oil
- 2 garlic cloves, minced
- ½ teaspoon dried oregano
- 2 teaspoons ground cumin
- ⅓ cup red pepper, minced
- ½ cup green olives, chopped
- ⅓ cup onion, minced
- 6 cups cauliflower rice
- Ground black pepper
- Salt

Directions:

1. Add meat in a large pot and cook over medium heat until meat is brown. Season with black pepper and salt. Remove meat from pot and set aside.
2. Add oil red pepper, onion, pepper, and salt in a pot and sauté for 2 minutes.
3. Add garlic and sauté for 30 seconds.

4. Add wine, water, bay leaf, tomato paste, tomatoes, olives, and spices and stir everything well.
5. Return meat to the pot and simmer over low heat for 15 minutes.
6. Remove meat mixture from pot and place on a plate.
7. Add cauliflower and butter in the same pot and cook for 5 minutes.
8. Serve ground meat over cauliflower.

Nutritional Value (Amount per Serving):

- Calories 289
- Fat 12 g
- Carbohydrates 6.7 g
- Sugar 3 g
- Protein 36.5 g
- Cholesterol 105 mg

Chipotle Beef Brisket

Preparation Time: 10 minutes

Cooking Time: 1 hour, 45 minutes

Serve: 4

Ingredients:

- 3½ pounds beef brisket, cut into pieces
- ¼ cup cilantro, chopped
- 1 cup chicken stock
- 2 tablespoons chipotle powder
- 1 tablespoon butter
- 1 teaspoon sea salt

Directions:

1. Add butter into the Instant Pot and set the pot on sauté mode.
2. Add brisket into the pot and sauté until lightly brown.
3. Add remaining ingredients and stir well.
4. Seal the pot with a lid and cook on Meat/Stew mode for 1 hour and 45 minutes.
5. Release pressure using quick release method than open the lid.
6. Slice and serve.

Nutritional Value (Amount per Serving):

- Calories 765
- Fat 27 g
- Carbohydrates 0.2 g
- Sugar 0.2 g
- Protein 120 g
- Cholesterol 362 mg

Beef Barbacoa

Preparation Time: 15 minutes

Cooking Time: 8 hours

Serve: 8

Ingredients:

- 3 pounds chuck roast, trimmed and cut into chunks
- 4 ounces can green chilies, chopped
- 2 chipotles, chopped
- ½ cup water
- ¼ teaspoon ground cloves
- 1 tablespoon dried oregano
- 1 tablespoon ground cumin
- 3 garlic cloves, minced
- 2 bay leaves
- 2 tablespoons apple cider vinegar
- ¼ cup fresh lime juice
- 1 cup onion, chopped
- ½ teaspoon black pepper
- 2 teaspoons salt

Directions:

1. Add all ingredients into the slow cooker and stir well.
2. Cover slow cooker and cook on low for 8 hours.
3. Remove meat from slow cooker and shred using a fork.
4. Return shredded meat to the slow cooker and stir well.
5. Serve and enjoy.

Nutritional Value (Amount per Serving):

- Calories 387

- Fat 14.4 g
- Carbohydrates 3.6 g
- Sugar 0.7 g
- Protein 56.7 g
- Cholesterol 172 mg

Spicy Beef

Preparation Time: 10 minutes

Cooking Time: 8 minutes

Serve: 4

Ingredients:

- 1 pound ground beef
- 1 teaspoon red pepper, crushed
- ½ teaspoon fresh ginger, minced
- 2 garlic cloves, minced
- 1 tablespoon olive oil
- 3 tablespoons green onion, sliced
- 3 tablespoons soy sauce
- ½ teaspoon stevia drops

Directions:

1. Heat olive oil in a pan over medium heat.
2. Add garlic and meat and cook until meat is brown about 6 minutes.
3. Add red pepper, ginger, soy sauce, and stevia. Mix well.
4. Stir for 2 minutes until well blended.
5. Garnish with green onion and serve.

Nutritional Value (Amount per Serving):

- Calories 264
- Fat 10.7 g
- Carbohydrates 4.9 g
- Sugar 2.3 g
- Protein 35.7 g
- Cholesterol 101 mg

Moist Shredded Pork

Preparation Time: 10 minutes

Cooking Time: 6 hours, 5 minutes

Serve: 8

Ingredients:

- 4 pounds pork roast, boneless, trimmed, and cut into chunks
- 1 teaspoon chili powder
- ½ teaspoon black pepper
- 2 teaspoons cumin
- 1 cup chicken stock
- 1 tablespoon chipotle powder
- 3 garlic cloves, minced
- 1 onion, diced
- 1½ teaspoons salt

Directions:

1. Add all ingredients into the slow cooker and stir well.
2. Cover slow cooker and cook on low for 6 hours.
3. Remove meat from slow cooker and shred using a fork.
4. Place shredded meat onto a baking tray and broil for 5 minutes.
5. Pour slow cooker sauce over broil meat and serve.

Nutritional Value (Amount per Serving):

- Calories 482
- Fat 21.7 g
- Carbohydrates 2.4 g
- Sugar 0.7 g
- Protein 65.1 g
- Cholesterol 195 mg

Lemon Pork Cutlet

Preparation Time: 10 minutes

Cooking Time: 20 minutes

Serve: 4

Ingredients:

- 1½ pounds pork, sliced thinly
- 1 fresh lemon juice
- ½ cup heavy cream
- 2 green onion, chopped
- 2 tablespoons butter
- Ground black pepper
- Salt

Directions:

1. Season pork with black pepper and salt.
2. In a small pan, melt 1 tablespoon butter over medium heat. Once butter melts, add onion and sauté for 4 minutes.
3. Add cream stir well and simmer for 10 minutes.
4. In another pan melt butter over medium-high heat. Once butter melts, add pork slices and cook for 2 minutes on each side.
5. Add fresh lemon juice in sauce and stir well.
6. Pour sauce over pork slices and serve.

Nutritional Value (Amount per Serving):

- Calories 348
- Fat 17.3 g
- Carbohydrates 1.0 g
- Sugar 0.2 g
- Protein 45.0 g

Beef Cabbage Skillet

Preparation Time: 10 minutes

Cooking Time: 20 minutes

Serve: 4

Ingredients:

- 1 pound ground beef
- 2 cups cabbage, shredded
- ½ cup salsa
- ¾ cup cheddar cheese, shredded
- 2 teaspoons chili powder
- Ground black pepper
- Salt

Directions:

1. Heat pan over medium heat.
2. Add meat in a pan and cook until brown. Drain excess fat.
3. Add cabbage, seasoning, and salsa to the pan and bring to boil.
4. Cover pan and turn heat to medium and cook for 10 minutes or until cabbage is softened.
5. Remove pan from heat and mix in cheddar cheese until melted.
6. Serve and enjoy.

Nutritional Value (Amount per Serving):

- Calories 318
- Fat 14.4 g
- Carbohydrates 5.1 g
- Sugar 2.3 g
- Protein 40.8 g
- Cholesterol 124 mg

Tasty Pork Tenderloin

Preparation Time: 10 minutes

Cooking Time: 35 minutes

Serve: 6

Ingredients:

- 2 pork tenderloins

For rub:

- 1 tablespoon onion powder
- 1 tablespoon smoked paprika
- 1 tablespoon garlic powder
- ½ tablespoon salt

Directions:

1. Preheat the oven to 425F/218C.
2. In a small bowl, combine all rub ingredients.
3. Coat pork tenderloin with the rub.
4. Heat ovenproof pan over medium-high heat.
5. Spray pan with cooking spray.
6. Sear pork on all sides until lightly golden brown.
7. Place pan into the preheated oven and roast for about 25 to 30 minutes.
8. Slice and serve.

Nutritional Value (Amount per Serving):

- Calories 194
- Fat 5 g
- Carbohydrates 2 g
- Sugar 0.9 g
- Protein 31 g

Lamb Roast

Preparation Time: 10 minutes

Cooking Time: 4 hours

Serve: 6

Ingredients:

- 4 pounds leg of lamb
- 4 tablespoons dried rosemary
- 4 garlic cloves, sliced
- 1 fresh lemon juice
- 1 tablespoon olive oil
- Ground black pepper
- Salt

Directions:

1. Make deep incision all over leg of lamb.
2. Push rosemary and garlic into the incisions and drizzle olive oil.
3. Season with black pepper and salt.
4. Place leg of lamb in slow cooker.
5. Pour lemon juice over leg of lamb.
6. Cook leg of lamb on high for 4 hours.
7. Slice and serve.

Nutritional Value (Amount per Serving):

- Calories 593
- Fat 24.8 g
- Carbohydrates 2.1 g
- Sugar 0.2 g
- Protein 85.1 g
- Cholesterol 272 mg

Spicy Lamb Chops

Preparation Time: 10 minutes

Cooking Time: 20 minutes

Serve: 5

Ingredients:

- 5 lamb rib chops
- ½ teaspoon smoked paprika
- 1 teaspoon cumin
- ½ tablespoon dried oregano
- 1 garlic clove, minced
- 2 tablespoons olive oil
- 1 teaspoon hot paprika

Directions:

1. In a small bowl, combine hot paprika, smoked paprika, cumin, oregano, garlic, and 1 tablespoon olive oil.
2. In mixing bowl, add lamb chops and paprika mixture rub until well coated and place in the refrigerator for 3 hours.
3. Preheat the oven at 350F/180C.
4. Heat remaining 1 tablespoon olive oil in an oven-safe pan over medium-high heat.
5. Once the oil is hot, then place lamb chops and cook for 3 minutes or until browned.
6. Place pan in preheated oven and cook for 8 minutes.
7. Turn chops to another side and cook for 8 minutes.
8. Serve and enjoy.

Nutritional Value (Amount per Serving):

- Calories 221
- Fat 12.4 g

- Carbohydrates 0.8 g
- Sugar 0.2 g
- Protein 25.7 g
- Cholesterol 82 mg

Chapter 9: Poultry

Flavors Chicken Tenders

Preparation Time: 5 minutes

Cooking Time: 15 minutes

Serve: 4

Ingredients:

- 1½ pounds chicken tenders
- 1 teaspoon rotisserie chicken seasoning
- 2 tablespoons homemade barbecue sauce
- 1 tablespoon extra-virgin olive oil

Directions:

1. Add all ingredients except oil in a resealable plastic bag.
2. Seal bag and place in the refrigerator for 2 to 3 hours.
3. Heat oil in a large pan over medium heat.
4. Cook marinated chicken tenders in a pan until lightly brown and cooked.
5. Serve and enjoy.

Nutritional Value (Amount per Serving):

- Calories 365
- Fat 16.1 g
- Carbohydrates 2.8 g
- Sugar 2 g
- Protein 49.2 g
- Cholesterol 151 mg

Mustard Chicken Tenders

Preparation Time: 10 minutes

Cooking Time: 20 minutes

Serve: 4

Ingredients:

- 1 pound chicken tenders
- ½ ounce fresh lemon juice
- 2 tablespoons fresh tarragon, chopped
- ½ cup whole grain mustard
- ½ teaspoon paprika
- 1 garlic clove, minced
- ½ teaspoon ground black pepper
- ¼ teaspoon kosher salt

Directions:

1. Preheat the oven to 425F/220C.
2. Add all ingredients except chicken to the large bowl and mix well.
3. Add chicken to the bowl and stir until well coated.
4. Place chicken on a baking dish and cover.
5. Place in preheated oven and cook for 15 to 20 minutes.
6. Serve and enjoy.

Nutritional Value (Amount per Serving):

- Calories 242
- Fat 9.5 g
- Carbohydrates 3.1 g
- Sugar 0.1 g
- Protein 33.2 g
- Cholesterol 101 mg

Chicken Chili

Preparation Time: 10 minutes

Cooking Time: 20 minutes

Serve: 8

Ingredients:

- 2½ pounds chicken breasts, skinless and boneless
- ½ teaspoon cumin powder
- 3 garlic cloves, minced
- 1 onion, diced
- 1 tablespoon olive oil
- 16 ounces salsa
- 1 teaspoon dried oregano

Directions:

1. Add oil into the Instant Pot and set the pot on sauté mode.
2. Add onion to the pot and sauté until softened, about 3 minutes.
3. Add garlic and sauté for a minute.
4. Add oregano and cumin and sauté for a minute.
5. Add half salsa and stir well.
6. Place chicken and pour remaining salsa over chicken.
7. Seal pot with lid and cook on manual mode for 10 minutes.
8. Release the pressure naturally, and then open the lid.
9. Remove chicken from pot and shred using a fork.
10. Return shredded chicken to the pot and stir well to combine.
11. Serve and enjoy.

Nutritional Value (Amount per Serving):

- Calories 308
- Fat 12.4 g

- Carbohydrates 5.4 g
- Sugar 2.3 g
- Protein 42.1 g
- Cholesterol 126 mg

Herb Chicken

Preparation Time: 10 minutes

Cooking Time: 25 minutes

Serve: 2

Ingredients:

- 1 pound chicken thighs
- 2 tablespoons lemon juice
- ⅛ teaspoon thyme, dried
- ½ teaspoon fresh rosemary, chopped
- 1 teaspoon garlic, minced
- 2 tablespoons white wine
- ½ cup tangerine juice
- Ground black pepper
- Salt

Directions:

1. Place chicken thighs into the bowl.
2. In another bowl, mix tangerine juice, garlic, white wine, lemon juice, thyme, rosemary, black pepper, and salt.
3. Pour over chicken thighs and place in the refrigerator for 20 minutes.
4. Preheat the oven at 450F/230C.
5. Spray a baking tray with cooking spray.
6. Arrange marinated chicken on baking tray and roast for 25 minutes.
7. Serve and enjoy.

Nutritional Value (Amount per Serving):

- Calories 473
- Fat 17.0 g
- Carbohydrates 7.4 g

- Sugar 6.0 g
- Protein 66.3 g
- Cholesterol 202 mg

Chili Chicken Wings

Preparation Time: 10 minutes

Cooking Time: 60 minutes

Serve: 4

Ingredients:

- 2 pounds chicken wings
- ⅛ teaspoon paprika
- 2 teaspoons seasoned salt
- ½ cup coconut flour
- ¼ teaspoon garlic powder
- ¼ teaspoon chili powder

Directions:

1. Preheat the oven to 400F/200C.
2. In a mixing bowl, add all ingredients except chicken wings and mix well.
3. Add chicken wings to the bowl mixture and coat well and place on a baking tray.
4. Bake in preheated oven for 60 minutes.
5. Serve and enjoy.

Nutritional Value (Amount per Serving):

- Calories 440
- Fat 17.1 g
- Carbohydrates 1.3 g
- Sugar 0.2 g
- Protein 65.9 g
- Cholesterol 202 mg

Garlic Zucchini Chicken Casserole

Preparation Time: 10 minutes

Cooking Time: 40 minutes

Serve: 8

Ingredients:

- 2½ pounds chicken breasts, boneless and cubed
- 5 zucchinis, cut into cubes
- 1 teaspoon xanthan gum
- 1 tablespoon tomato paste
- 5.4 ounces coconut cream
- 12 ounces roasted red peppers, drained and chopped
- 10 garlic cloves
- ⅔ cup mayonnaise
- 1 teaspoon salt

Directions:

1. Preheat the oven to 400F/200C.
2. Add zucchini and chicken to a casserole dish. Cover dish with aluminum foil.
3. Bake in preheated oven for 25 minutes. Stir well and cook for 10 minutes more.
4. Meanwhile, in a bowl, stir together remaining ingredients.
5. Pour bowl mixture over chicken and zucchini and broil on high for 5 minutes.
6. Serve and enjoy.

Nutritional Value (Amount per Serving):

- Calories 235
- Fat 14.9 g
- Carbohydrates 11.4 g
- Sugar 5.8 g
- Protein 16 g

Chicken Cumin Wings

Preparation Time: 10 minutes

Cooking Time: 45 minutes

Serve: 6

Ingredients:

- 12 chicken wings
- 2 garlic cloves, minced
- 3 tablespoons clarified butter
- ½ teaspoon turmeric
- 2 teaspoons cumin seeds
- ½ teaspoon black pepper
- ½ teaspoon salt

Directions:

1. Preheat the oven to 425F/ 215 C.
2. In a large bowl, mix 1 teaspoon cumin, 1 tablespoon butter, turmeric, pepper, and salt.
3. Add chicken wings to the bowl and toss until well coated.
4. Spread chicken wings on a baking tray and bake in preheated oven for 30 minutes.
5. Turn chicken wings to the other side and bake for 8 minutes more.
6. Meanwhile, heat remaining butter in a pan over medium heat.
7. Add garlic and cumin to the pan and cook for 1 minute.
8. Remove pan from heat and set aside.
9. Remove chicken wings from the oven and spoon ghee mixture over each chicken wing.
10. Bake chicken wings 5 minutes more.
11. Serve and enjoy.

Nutritional Value (Amount per Serving):

- Calories 378

- Fat 27.9 g
- Carbohydrates 11.4 g
- Sugar 0 g
- Protein 19.7 g
- Cholesterol 94 mg

Chicken Cheese Casserole

Preparation Time: 10 minutes

Cooking Time: 40 minutes

Serve: 8

Ingredients:

- 2 pounds cooked chicken, shredded
- 6 ounces cream cheese, softened
- 4 ounces butter, melted
- 5 ounces Swiss cheese
- 1 ounce fresh lemon juice
- 1 tablespoon Dijon mustard
- 6 ounces ham, cut into small pieces
- ½ teaspoon salt

Directions:

1. Preheat the oven to 350F/176C.
2. Arrange chicken in the bottom of a baking dish then layer ham pieces on top.
3. Add butter, lemon juice, mustard, cream cheese, and salt into the blender and blend until a thick sauce.
4. Spread sauce over top of chicken and ham mixture in the baking dish.
5. Arrange Swiss cheese slices on top of sauce and bake in preheated oven for 40 minutes.

Nutritional Value (Amount per Serving):

- Calories 451
- Fat 29.2 g
- Carbohydrates 2.5 g
- Sugar 0.4 g
- Protein 43 g

Chicken With Mushrooms

Preparation Time: 10 minutes

Cooking Time: 30 minutes

Serve: 4

Ingredients:

- 2 pounds chicken breasts, halved
- 8 ounces mushrooms, sliced
- ½ cup mayonnaise
- ⅓ cup sundried tomatoes
- 1 teaspoon salt

Directions:

1. Preheat the oven to 400F/204C.
2. Grease baking dish with butter.
3. Place chicken breasts into the baking dish and top with sundried tomatoes, mushrooms, mayonnaise, and salt. Mix well.
4. Bake chicken in preheated oven for 30 minutes.
5. Serve and enjoy.

Nutritional Value (Amount per Serving):

- Calories 560
- Fat 26.8 g
- Carbohydrates 9.5 g
- Sugar 3.2 g
- Protein 67.8 g
- Cholesterol 209 mg

Spicy Chicken Curry

Preparation Time: 10 minutes

Cooking Time: 40 minutes

Serve: 6

Ingredients:

- 2 pounds chicken legs, wash and clean
- 1 scallion stalk, sliced
- 2 tablespoons Jamaican curry powder
- 1 tablespoon seasoning salt
- 1 thyme sprig
- ½ medium onion, sliced

Directions:

1. Season chicken with seasoning salt.
2. Spray pan with cooking spray and heat over medium heat.
3. Add curry powder, thyme, onion, and scallion to the pan and stir well.
4. Add chicken to the pan and cook until chicken is brown, about 10 minutes on high heat.
5. Add 2 cups water and stir well. Cover and simmer for 30 minutes.
6. Stir well and serve.

Nutritional Value (Amount per Serving):

- Calories 291
- Fat 11.2 g
- Carbohydrates 0.9 g
- Sugar 0.4 g
- Protein 43.8 g
- Cholesterol 135 mg

Chapter 10: Seafood

Tomato Lemon Fish Fillet

Preparation Time: 10 minutes

Cooking Time: 13 minutes

Serve: 6

Ingredients:

- 1½ pounds cod fillet
- 28 ounces canned diced tomatoes
- 1 lemon juice
- 3 tablespoons coconut oil
- 1 teaspoon dried oregano
- 1 onion, sliced
- ½ teaspoon ground black pepper
- 1 teaspoon salt

Directions:

1. Add oil into the Instant Pot and set the pot on sauté mode.
2. Add remaining ingredients into the pot and sauté for 8 minutes.
3. Seal pot with lid and cook on high pressure for 5 minutes.
4. Release pressure using quick release method than open the lid.
5. Serve and enjoy.

Nutritional Value (Amount per Serving):

- Calories 186
- Fat 7.9 g
- Carbohydrates 8.7 g
- Protein 21.7 g
- Sugar 5.3 g

Turmeric Coconut Shrimp

Preparation Time: 10 minutes

Cooking Time: 4 minutes

Serve: 4

Ingredients:

- 1 pound shrimp, deveined
- ½ teaspoon cayenne pepper
- ½ teaspoon turmeric
- 1 tablespoon ginger, minced
- 1 tablespoon garlic, minced
- 6.5 ounces coconut milk, unsweetened
- 1 teaspoon garam masala
- 1 teaspoon salt

Directions:

1. Add all ingredients into the microwave-safe bowl. Stir well.
2. Cover bowl with foil. Pour 1 cup water into the Instant Pot then place trivet into the pot.
3. Place bowl on a trivet. Seal pot with lid and cook on low pressure for 4 minutes.
4. Release pressure using quick release method than open the lid.
5. Serve and enjoy.

Nutritional Value (Amount per Serving):

- Calories 250
- Fat 13 g
- Carbohydrates 6.2 g
- Sugar 1.6 g
- Protein 27 g
- Cholesterol 239 mg

Rosemary Lemon Salmon

Preparation Time: 10 minutes

Cooking Time: 2 hours

Serve: 2

Ingredients:

- 8 ounces salmon
- 1 fresh lemon, sliced
- 2 tablespoons lemon juice
- ⅓ cup water
- ¼ teaspoon fresh rosemary, minced
- 1 tablespoon capers

Directions:

1. Place salmon into the slow cooker.
2. Pour lemon juice and water over salmon.
3. Arrange lemon slices over the top of salmon.
4. Sprinkle with rosemary and capers.
5. Cover and cook on low for 2 hours.
6. Serve and enjoy.

Nutritional Value (Amount per Serving):

- Calories 164
- Fat 7.3 g
- Carbohydrates 3.3 g
- Sugar 1.1 g
- Protein 22.6 g
- Cholesterol 50 mg

Ginger Lime Salmon

Preparation Time: 10 minutes

Cooking Time: 3 minutes

Serve: 12

Ingredients:

- 3 pounds salmon fillet, remove bones
- ¼ cup lime juice
- ¼ cup fresh ginger, minced
- 1 onion, sliced
- 1 lime, sliced

Directions:

1. Place salmon skin side down into the slow cooker.
2. Pour lime juice over the salmon then add ginger.
3. Arrange lime and onion slices over the salmon.
4. Cover and cook on low for 3 hours.
5. Serve and enjoy.

Nutritional Value (Amount per Serving):

- Calories 166
- Fat 7.2 g
- Carbohydrates 4.1 g
- Sugar 0.8 g
- Protein 22.4 g
- Cholesterol 50 mg

Shrimp Scampi

Preparation Time: 10 minutes

Cooking Time: 13 minutes

Serve: 4

Ingredients:

- 1 pound shrimp, peeled and deveined
- 10 garlic cloves, peeled
- 2 tablespoons olive oil
- ¼ cup Parmesan cheese, grated
- 2 tablespoons butter, melted
- 1 fresh lemon, cut into wedges

Directions:

1. Preheat the oven to 400F/200C.
2. Combine shrimp, lemon wedges, olive oil, and garlic cloves on a baking tray. Toss well.
3. Bake in preheated oven for 13 minutes or until shrimp is opaque.
4. Remove baking tray from the oven.
5. Drizzle with melted butter and sprinkle with Parmesan cheese.
6. Serve and enjoy.

Nutritional Value (Amount per Serving):

- Calories 297
- Fat 17 g
- Carbohydrates 4.7 g
- Sugar 0.1 g
- Protein 29.5 g
- Cholesterol 262 mg

Chili Lemon Salmon

Preparation Time: 10 minutes

Cooking Time: 22 minutes

Serve: 4

Ingredients:

- 2 pounds salmon fillet, skinless and boneless
- 2 lemon juice
- 1 orange juice
- 1 tablespoon olive oil
- 1 bunch fresh dill
- 1 chili, sliced
- Ground black pepper
- Salt

Directions:

1. Preheat the oven to 350F/176C.
2. Place salmon fillet on a baking tray and drizzle with olive oil, lemon juice, and orange juice.
3. Sprinkle chili slices over the salmon and season with black pepper and salt.
4. Roast in preheated oven for 22 minutes.
5. Garnish with dill and serve.

Nutritional Value (Amount per Serving):

- Calories 340
- Fat 17.5 g
- Carbohydrates 2.3 g
- Sugar 1.8 g
- Protein 44.2 g
- Cholesterol 100 mg

Parmesan Salmon

Preparation Time: 10 minutes

Cooking Time: 15 minutes

Serve: 4

Ingredients:

- 4 salmon fillets
- ¼ cup Parmesan cheese, grated
- ½ cup walnuts
- 1 teaspoon olive oil
- 1 tablespoon lemon rind

Directions:

1. Preheat the oven to 400F/200C.
2. Spray a baking tray with cooking spray.
3. Place salmon on a baking tray.
4. Add walnuts into the grinder and process until finely ground.
5. Mix ground walnuts with Parmesan cheese, oil, and lemon rind. Stir well.
6. Spoon walnut mixture over the salmon fillets and press gently.
7. Bake in preheated oven for 15 minutes.
8. Serve and enjoy.

Nutritional Value (Amount per Serving):

- Calories 423
- Fat 27.4 g
- Carbohydrates 1.9 g
- Sugar 0.3 g
- Protein 46.3 g
- Cholesterol 98 mg

Shrimp and Grits

Preparation Time: 10 minutes

Cooking Time: 7 minutes

Serve: 6

Ingredients:

- 1 pound shrimp, thawed
- ½ cup quick grits
- 1 teaspoon paprika
- 2 tablespoons cilantro, chopped
- ½ cup cheddar cheese, shredded
- 1 tablespoon coconut oil
- 1 tablespoon butter
- 1 ½ cups chicken broth
- ¼ teaspoon red pepper flakes
- ½ teaspoon kosher salt

Directions:

1. Add oil into the Instant Pot and set the pot on sauté mode.
2. Add shrimp into the pot and cook until it turns to pink. Season with red pepper flakes and salt.
3. Remove shrimp from the pot and set aside.
4. Add remaining ingredients into the pot and mix well.
5. Seal pot with lid and cook on manual high pressure for 7 minutes.
6. Release the pressure naturally, and then open the lid.
7. Add cheese and stir until cheese melted.
8. Top with shrimp and serve.

Nutritional Value (Amount per Serving):

- Calories 222

- Fat 9 g
- Carbohydrates 12 g
- Sugar 0.3 g
- Protein 21 g
- Cholesterol 174 mg

Chapter 11: Soup & Sides

Cabbage Coconut Soup

Preparation Time: 10 minutes

Cooking Time: 30 minutes

Serve: 4

Ingredients:

- 1 small cabbage head
- 2 tablespoons coconut oil
- 3 cups vegetable stock
- ¼ cup coconut milk
- 1 teaspoon cumin powder
- 2 teaspoons turmeric powder
- 2 garlic cloves, chopped
- ½ teaspoon black pepper
- ½ teaspoon salt

Directions:

1. Heat oil in a saucepan over medium heat.
2. Add cabbage and garlic and sauté for 10 minutes.
3. Add stock and stir well. Bring to boil and simmer for 20 minutes.
4. Remove from heat and add coconut milk and spices. Stir well.
5. Puree the soup using a blender until smooth and creamy.
6. Serve and enjoy.

Nutritional Value (Amount per Serving):

- Calories 149
- Fat 11.3 g
- Carbohydrates 13.3 g

- Sugar 6.8 g
- Protein 2.9 g
- Cholesterol 0 mg

Garlic Avocado Soup

Preparation Time: 10 minutes

Cooking Time: 10 minutes

Serve: 4

Ingredients:

- 2 avocados, pitted
- 4 cups chicken stock
- ½ pound bacon, cooked and chopped
- ½ lime juice
- 1 teaspoon garlic powder
- ⅓ cup fresh cilantro, chopped
- Ground black pepper
- Salt

Directions:

1. Add the stock into the saucepan and bring to boil.
2. Add avocados, lime juice, garlic powder, and cilantro into the blender.
3. Add 1 cup warm chicken stock into the blender and blend until smooth.
4. Remove saucepan from heat. Add avocado mixture and bacon into the saucepan and mix well.
5. Season with black pepper and salt.
6. Serve and enjoy.

Nutritional Value (Amount per Serving):

- Calories 351
- Fat 26.8 g
- Carbohydrates 4.1 g
- Sugar 1 g
- Protein 22.4 g

Broccoli Avocado Soup

Preparation Time: 10 minutes

Cooking Time: 12 minutes

Serve: 3

Ingredients:

- 4 cup broccoli florets
- 1 small avocado, peel and sliced
- ½ teaspoon nutmeg
- 2 cups vegetable broth

Directions:

1. Add broth into the pot and bring to simmer over medium-high heat.
2. Add broccoli into the pot and cook for 8 minutes.
3. Reduce heat to low and add avocado and nutmeg.
4. Stir well and cooks for 4 minutes.
5. Puree the soup using a blender until smooth.
6. Serve and enjoy.

Nutritional Value (Amount per Serving):

- Calories 89
- Fat 3.1 g
- Carbohydrates 9.9 g
- Sugar 2.6 g
- Protein 7 g
- Cholesterol 0 mg

Roasted Mushrooms

Preparation Time: 10 minutes

Cooking Time: 45 minutes

Serve: 4

Ingredients:

- 8 ounces mushrooms, sliced
- 2 tablespoons olive oil
- 2 onions, sliced
- ½ teaspoon thyme
- 2 tablespoons balsamic vinegar

Directions:

1. Preheat the oven to 375 F/190C.
2. Line baking tray with aluminum foil and spray with cooking spray and set aside.
3. In a mixing bowl, add all ingredients and mix well.
4. Spread mushroom mixture onto a prepared baking tray.
5. Roast in preheated oven for 45 minutes.
6. Season with black pepper and salt.
7. Serve and enjoy.

Nutritional Value (Amount per Serving):

- Calories 96
- Fat 7.2 g
- Carbohydrates 7.2 g
- Sugar 3.3 g
- Protein 2.4 g
- Cholesterol 0 mg

Healthy Turmeric Broccoli Soup

Preparation Time: 10 minutes

Cooking Time: 3 hours, 10 minutes

Serve: 8

Ingredients:

- 8 cups broccoli florets
- 1 tablespoon olive oil
- 1 teaspoon turmeric
- 6 cup vegetable broth
- 2 tablespoons ginger, chopped
- 2 cups leeks, chopped
- 2 tablespoons butter
- 1 teaspoon salt

Directions:

1. Melt butter in a pan over medium heat.
2. Add leeks to the pan and sauté for 10 minutes.
3. Transfer leek and remaining ingredients into the slow cooker and stir well.
4. Cover slow cooker with lid and cook on low for 3 hours.
5. Puree the soup using a blender until smooth.
6. Serve and enjoy.

Nutritional Value (Amount per Serving):

- Calories 120
- Fat 6.1 g
- Carbohydrates 11 g
- Sugar 3 g
- Protein 6.7 g
- Cholesterol 8 mg

Cauliflower Mash

Preparation Time: 10 minutes

Cooking Time: 20 minutes

Serve: 4

Ingredients:

- 6 cups cauliflower florets
- 2 scallions, chopped
- 3 garlic cloves, crushed
- ⅓ cup coconut milk
- 3 cups kale, chopped
- 4 teaspoons coconut oil, melted
- Ground black pepper
- Salt

Directions:

1. Boil cauliflower florets into the boiling water until tender.
2. Drain cauliflower well and set aside.
3. Heat oil in a pan over medium-high heat.
4. Add scallions and garlic and sauté for 30 seconds.
5. Add kale and salt and cook until kale is wilted. Transfer kale mixture into the mixing bowl.
6. Add cauliflower and coconut milk into the blender and blend until smooth.
7. Add cauliflower mixture into the kale mixture and mix well. Season with black pepper and salt.
8. Serve and enjoy.

Nutritional Value (Amount per Serving):

- Calories 83
- Fat 5.6 g

- Carbohydrates 5.9 g
- Sugar 1 g
- Protein 2.7 g
- Cholesterol 0 mg

Spinach Cauliflower Green Soup

Preparation Time: 10 minutes

Cooking Time: 15 minutes

Serve: 4

Ingredients:

- 2 cups baby spinach, wash and pat dry
- ½ teaspoon ginger, grated
- ½ onion, diced
- 2 cups cauliflower florets
- 1 cup parsley, chopped
- 1 tablespoon olive oil
- 1 tablespoon coconut cream
- 2 cups vegetable stock

Directions:

1. Heat olive oil in a saucepan over medium heat.
2. Add onion and sauté until softened.
3. Add cauliflower and cook until softened.
4. Add vegetable stock and stir well.
5. Cover the saucepan with a lid and bring to boil.
6. Once the vegetable is softened, then add spinach, coconut cream, ginger, and parsley. Stir until spinach wilted.
7. Remove saucepan from heat and blend the soup with a blender until smooth.

Nutritional Value (Amount per Serving):

- Calories 71
- Fat 5.6 g
- Carbohydrates 6.8 g
- Sugar 3.1 g
- Protein 2.1 g

Garlic String Beans

Preparation Time: 5 minutes

Cooking Time: 6 minutes

Serve: 4

Ingredients:

- 1 pound fresh string beans, washed and ends trimmed
- 2 tablespoons olive oil
- 4 garlic cloves, sliced
- Ground black pepper
- Salt

Directions:

1. Add water in a large saucepan and bring to boil over medium heat.
2. Add beans in lower a steamer basket.
3. Cover pan and steam for 5 minutes or until beans are tender. Drain well.
4. Heat olive oil in a pan over medium heat.
5. Add garlic in a pan and sauté for a minute.
6. Add beans and season with black pepper and salt.
7. Toss well and serve.

Nutritional Value (Amount per Serving):

- Calories 100
- Fat 7.2 g
- Carbohydrates 9.1 g
- Sugar 1.6 g
- Protein 2.3 g
- Cholesterol 0 mg

Chapter 12: Desserts

Pecan Carrot Cake

Preparation Time: 10 minutes

Cooking Time: 45 minutes

Serve: 8

Ingredients:

- 4 eggs
- 1 cup pecan, chopped
- 2¼ cup carrots, grated
- ¼ teaspoon nutmeg
- 1½ cup coconut flour
- 1 teaspoon vanilla extract
- ¾ cup coconut oil, melted
- 1 tablespoon cinnamon
- 1 tablespoon baking powder
- 1 cup almond flour
- ½ cup stevia
- Pinch of salt

Directions:

1. Spray 7-inch cake pan with cooking spray and set aside.
2. Pour 2 cups water into the Instant Pot then place a trivet in the pot.
3. In a mixing bowl, mix sweetener, vanilla, and coconut oil.
4. Add eggs and stir well to combine.
5. Add coconut flour, nutmeg, cinnamon, baking powder, almond flour, and salt and stir to combine.
6. Add grated carrots and pecans and stir well.
7. Pour batter in the prepared cake pan.

8. Cover cake pan with aluminum foil piece and place on top of the trivet.
9. Seal pot with lid and cook on steam mode for 45 minutes.
10. Release pressure using quick release method than open the lid.
11. Remove cake from the pot and let it cool completely.
12. Slice and serve.

Nutritional Value (Amount per Serving):

- Calories 412
- Fat 40.1 g
- Carbohydrates 11.4 g
- Sugar 3 g
- Protein 7.9 g
- Cholesterol 82 mg

Choco Almond Bombs

Preparation Time: 10 minutes

Cooking Time: 5 minutes

Serve: 12

Ingredients:

- ¼ cup almonds, chopped
- 1 teaspoon stevia
- 4 tablespoons chocolate, melted and unsweetened
- ¼ cup butter
- ¼ cup coconut oil
- ¼ cup almond butter

Directions:

1. Add coconut oil, almond butter, and butter in a bowl mix well and microwave it for 30 seconds or until melted.
2. Add stevia, chopped almond, and melted chocolate. Mix well until combined.
3. Pour mixture into the silicone mold and place in the refrigerator for 1 hour or until set.
4. Serve and enjoy.

Nutritional Value (Amount per Serving):

- Calories 105
- Fat 10.9 g
- Carbohydrates 1.6 g
- Sugar 0.4 g
- Protein 1.3 g
- Cholesterol 0 mg

Vanilla Almond Balls

Preparation Time: 10 minutes

Cooking Time: 5 minutes

Serve: 8

Ingredients:

- 1 cup almond flour
- 1 teaspoon vanilla extract
- 2 tablespoons Swerve
- 3 tablespoons coconut oil, melted
- ⅛ teaspoon salt

Directions:

1. In a bowl, mix all ingredients until well combined.
2. Make small round balls from mixture and place onto a baking tray.
3. Place in refrigerator for 1 hour.
4. Serve and enjoy.

Nutritional Value (Amount per Serving):

- Calories 67
- Fat 6.9 g
- Carbohydrates 1.3 g
- Sugar 0.2 g
- Protein 0.8 g
- Cholesterol 0 mg

Choco Coconut Almond Muffins

Preparation Time: 10 minutes

Cooking Time: 10 minutes

Serve: 6

Ingredients:

- 2 eggs
- ¼ cup Swerve
- 3 tablespoons yogurt
- ¼ cup cream cheese
- 1 cup shredded coconut
- 1½ cups almond flour
- 1 teaspoon vanilla extract
- ¼ cup blueberries
- 2 teaspoons baking powder
- 3 tablespoons butter
- 2 tablespoons unsweetened cocoa powder

Directions:

1. In a large bowl, add butter and eggs and beat until fluffy.
2. Add Swerve, yogurt, and cream cheese and stir well.
3. Add almond flour, baking powder, and shredded coconut. Mix well.
4. Add blueberries and fold well.
5. Pour batter into the silicone muffin mold and set aside.
6. Pour 1 cup water into the Instant Pot and place trivet in the pot.
7. Place silicon mold on top of the trivet.
8. Seal pot with lid and cook on high for 10 minutes.
9. Release pressure using quick release method than open the lid.
10. Serve and enjoy.

Nutritional Value (Amount per Serving):

- Calories 330
- Fat 29.4 g
- Carbohydrates 11.7 g
- Sugar 3.2 g
- Protein 9.9 g
- Cholesterol 81 mg

Smooth Lemon Mousse

Preparation Time: 5 minutes

Cooking Time: 5 minutes

Serve: 2

Ingredients:

- 13.5 ounces coconut milk
- 12 drops liquid stevia
- ½ teaspoon lemon extract
- ¼ teaspoon turmeric

Directions:

1. Place coconut milk can in the refrigerator for overnight.
2. Scoop out thick cream into a mixing bowl.
3. Add remaining ingredients to the bowl and whip using a hand mixer until smooth.
4. Transfer mousse mixture to a resealable plastic bag and pipe into small serving glasses.
5. Place in refrigerator. Serve chilled and enjoy.

Nutritional Value (Amount per Serving):

- Calories 444
- Fat 45.7 g
- Carbohydrates 10 g
- Sugar 6 g
- Protein 4.4 g
- Cholesterol 0 mg

Lime Bites

Preparation Time: 5 minutes

Cooking Time: 5 minutes

Serve: 16

Ingredients:

For crust:

- ¼ cup macadamia nuts
- 2 tablespoons coconut sugar
- 1 teaspoon lime zest
- ⅛ teaspoon salt

For bites:

- ¼ cup Swerve
- ⅓ cup coconut oil, melted
- 1 teaspoon lime zest
- 3 tablespoons lime juice
- ½ cup sunflower seeds
- ½ cup macadamia nuts
- 1 tablespoon coconut flour
- ¼ cup unsweetened coconut milk

Directions:

1. Add all crust ingredients into the food processor and process until coarse. Pour into a bowl and set aside.
2. Add bites ingredients into the food processor and process until thick and creamy.
3. Spray candy mold tray with cooking spray.
4. Fill candy mold tray with creamy bites mixture and place in the refrigerator for 35 to 45 minutes or until firm.

5. Remove bites from mold and coat with pie crust.
6. Serve and enjoy.

Nutritional Value (Amount per Serving):

- Calories 144
- Fat 13.9 g
- Carbohydrates 8.7 g
- Sugar 4.4 g
- Protein 1.6 g
- Cholesterol 0 mg

Blueberry Lemon Cheesecake

Preparation Time: 10 minutes

Cooking Time: 30 minutes

Serve: 8

Ingredients:

- 4 eggs
- 2 tablespoons blueberries
- 16 ounces cream cheese
- ¼ cup coconut oil
- ½ cup almond flour
- 1 tablespoon erythritol
- ½ cup heavy whipping cream
- ¼ cup lemon juice
- 1 cup erythritol

Directions:

1. Line 7-inch spring-form pan with parchment paper and set aside.
2. In a bowl, combine almond flour, coconut oil, and 1 tablespoon erythritol.
3. Press almond flour mixture into the bottom of the spring-form pan.
4. In a large bowl, add cream cheese, 1 cup erythritol, and heavy cream and beat using a hand mixer until smooth.
5. Add lemon juice and stir well.
6. Add eggs and stir until well combined.
7. Add blueberries and fold well.
8. Pour cheese mixture into the pan over the crust.
9. Pour 1 cup water into the Instant Pot then place a trivet in the pot.
10. Cover cake pan with foil and place on top of the trivet.
11. Seal pot with lid and cook on manual mode for 30 minutes.
12. Release the pressure naturally, and then open the lid.
13. Remove cake pan from the pot and let it cool completely.

14. Place in refrigerator for 4 to 5 hours.
15. Slice and serve.

Nutritional Value (Amount per Serving):

- Calories 357
- Fat 35.1 g
- Carbohydrates 3.9 g
- Sugar 0.9 g
- Protein 8.8 g
- Cholesterol 154 mg

Chocolate Fudge

Preparation Time: 5 minutes

Cooking Time: 5 minutes

Serve: 12

Ingredients:

- 4 ounces unsweetened dark chocolate
- 1 teaspoon vanilla extract
- ¾ cup coconut butter
- 15 drops liquid stevia

Directions:

1. Melt coconut butter and dark chocolate.
2. Add ingredients to the large bowl and combine well.
3. Pour mixture into a silicone loaf pan and place in refrigerator until solidified.
4. Remove from pan and cut into pieces.
5. Serve and enjoy.

Nutritional Value (Amount per Serving):

- Calories 157
- Fat 14.1 g
- Carbohydrates 6.1 g
- Sugar 1 g
- Protein 2.3 g
- Cholesterol 0 mg

Conclusion

This book is perfect for ketogenic diet beginners. You will get everything in this book that allows you to not only prepare keto-friendly recipes but also understand the principles behind the keto diet. In this book, you will find 64 delicious and healthy keto recipes that are easy to prepare.

59366032R00062

Made in the USA
Middletown, DE
10 August 2019